Beyond the Algorithm

Understanding Artificial Intelligence, Machine Learning, and Deep Learning Like Never Before

What You Need to Know About AI, ML, and

DL - The Technologies Shaping the Future

Joe E. Grayson

Table of Contents

Introduction

Artificial Intelligence has emerged as one of the most transformative technologies of our time, shaping the way we live, work, and interact with the world around us. Its rapid evolution has brought about innovations that were once the realm of science fiction, from virtual assistants capable of understanding and responding to human language to self-driving cars navigating complex traffic patterns. Every day, AI finds new applications in industries like healthcare, finance, entertainment, and even creative arts, revolutionizing traditional practices and opening up possibilities we never imagined.

Understanding AI is no longer just the domain of researchers and technologists; it is becoming a necessity for everyone. Whether we realize it or not, AI is deeply embedded in our daily routines. It powers the recommendation systems suggesting what we should watch next, optimizes navigation routes, enhances the quality of medical diagnoses, and even detects fraud in financial transactions. Despite its growing presence, there are still widespread misconceptions about what AI truly is and how it works. Many confuse it with Machine Learning or Deep Learning, while others view it as an all-knowing, autonomous force capable of replacing human intelligence. The truth lies somewhere in between, and untangling these misconceptions is crucial for appreciating its potential and understanding its limitations.

The goal of this book is to provide readers with a clear and comprehensive understanding of Artificial Intelligence, Machine Learning, and Deep Learning, regardless of their prior familiarity with these topics. By breaking down complex ideas into straightforward explanations, this book aims to make AI accessible to everyone, whether you are a professional looking to leverage AI in your field or simply a curious reader wanting to understand the technology shaping the future.

Through this exploration, we will uncover how these systems work, why they matter, and how they are transforming the way we live. The intention is not just to inform but to empower readers to engage with these technologies in meaningful ways, preparing them to navigate an AI-driven world with confidence and insight.

Chapter 1: What Is Artificial Intelligence?

Artificial Intelligence can be simply defined as the replication or enhancement of human intelligence in machines. At its core, AI aims to emulate the way humans think, learn, and solve problems. It is about enabling systems to perform tasks that would normally require human intelligence, such as understanding language, recognizing patterns, making decisions, or even discovering new information. Unlike traditional programming, which relies on explicitly defined rules, AI systems are designed to adapt and learn, mimicking human capabilities in increasingly sophisticated ways.

The essence of AI can be captured in three fundamental pillars: discovery, inference, and reasoning. Discovery refers to the ability of AI to uncover new insights from data, identifying patterns or relationships that might not be immediately apparent. Inference involves drawing conclusions from incomplete or implicit information, much like how humans can "read between the lines" to understand what is not directly stated. Reasoning, the final pillar, enables AI systems to combine existing knowledge in innovative ways, allowing them to derive new insights or solutions to problems.

The scope of AI goes far beyond simple computations. Traditional computer programs are excellent at following rules to perform specific tasks, but AI takes this a step further by mimicking human-like problem-solving. For instance, AI systems can process visual information, enabling them to "see" and analyze images or videos, a capability known as computer vision. They can also understand and generate human language, a field called natural language processing. Additionally, robotics integrates AI with physical motion, enabling machines to perform tasks like navigating environments, lifting objects, or even performing intricate movements such as tying shoelaces.

Despite its advancements, AI is often misunderstood. Many people associate AI exclusively with humanoid robots or futuristic scenarios depicted in science fiction. While robots can be powered by AI, they represent only one small aspect of this vast field. AI is not a singular entity or a standalone technology but rather a collection of techniques and systems designed to solve problems and improve efficiency. Dispelling these myths is essential to appreciating the real-world impact and practical applications of AI. Far from being confined to the realm of fantasy, AI is a powerful and versatile tool that is already reshaping industries and redefining how we interact with technology.

Chapter 2: The Building Blocks of AI

In the context of machines, intelligence refers to the ability of a system to perform tasks that require understanding, adaptation, and decision-making. Unlike conventional software, which follows rigidly defined rules, AI systems are designed to mimic the human capacity to learn, reason, and solve problems. Intelligence in machines is not about consciousness or emotions; rather, it is about replicating the processes that allow humans to analyze situations, draw conclusions, and act effectively in a variety of circumstances.

AI systems achieve this by learning from data. Learning in AI involves processing vast amounts of information to identify patterns, relationships, and trends. By doing so, these systems can make predictions, adapt to new inputs, and improve their performance over time. This simulation of human thinking relies on models and algorithms that are designed to handle complex problems in a way that mimics how humans approach reasoning and decision-making.

Data serves as the foundation for this learning process. AI systems thrive on data, much like humans rely on experience to improve their understanding of the world. Large datasets are critical because they provide the variety and volume needed to train AI models effectively. The more diverse and comprehensive the data, the better the system becomes at recognizing patterns and making accurate predictions. For instance, an AI system designed for language translation requires exposure to countless examples of text in multiple languages to understand context, grammar, and meaning.

Without sufficient data, AI systems would lack the insights needed to perform effectively, underscoring the importance of robust, high-quality datasets.

The design of AI systems involves a careful balance between algorithms, programming, and learning. Algorithms are the step-by-step processes or rules that guide how an AI system analyzes and processes data. Programming provides the initial structure and logic for the system to operate. However, the distinguishing feature of AI lies in its capacity for learning. Instead of relying solely on predefined rules, AI systems use machine learning techniques to refine their behavior based on data. This approach allows them to adapt dynamically and handle tasks beyond the scope of their original programming.

By blending these elements—intelligence, data, and design—AI systems are able to simulate human-like problem-solving in increasingly sophisticated ways. This ability to learn, adapt, and improve makes AI a transformative force, capable of addressing challenges that were once thought to be the exclusive domain of human intelligence.

Chapter 3: Machine Learning (ML) Demystified

Machine Learning represents a significant departure from traditional programming by moving away from explicit instructions and instead relying on data-driven learning. In traditional programming, every task requires a developer to write specific code that dictates how the system should function. If new requirements arise, the program must be rewritten or modified to address those changes. Machine Learning, in contrast, allows systems to learn and adapt by analyzing data, eliminating the need for constant manual intervention. By recognizing patterns and drawing insights from vast amounts of information, Machine Learning enables systems to make predictions and decisions with increasing accuracy over time.

At its core, Machine Learning can be viewed as a sophisticated form of statistical analysis. It builds models that process data, identify trends, and make sense of complex relationships. What sets it apart from conventional statistical methods is its focus on automation and scalability. Instead of merely interpreting static datasets, Machine Learning models improve as they are exposed to more data, enabling them to refine their predictions and enhance their functionality autonomously.

One of the most distinctive features of Machine Learning is its ability to make predictions and decisions based on the data it processes. For example, a machine learning model might analyze a user's browsing habits to recommend a product or predict the likelihood of fraudulent activity in financial transactions. This adaptability is another hallmark of Machine Learning. Rather than being static tools, these models evolve as they ingest new information, adapting their outputs to reflect changes in patterns or contexts.

Machine Learning comes in two primary forms: supervised learning and unsupervised learning. Supervised learning relies on human-labeled data and oversight during the training process. For instance, in a supervised learning model designed to classify images of cats and dogs, the training data would include images explicitly labeled as "cat" or "dog." The system learns to associate features in the data with the correct labels, enabling it to make accurate classifications when presented with new, unlabeled examples. On the other hand, unsupervised learning does not require labeled data. Instead, it autonomously identifies patterns, clusters, or structures within the data. For example, an unsupervised model might analyze customer purchase behavior to group similar users based on buying habits, even without explicit instructions on what those groups represent.

Machine Learning is a subset of Artificial Intelligence, focusing specifically on the ability to learn from data. While AI encompasses a broad range of technologies designed to mimic human intelligence, Machine Learning is one of its most prominent components. The practical applications of Machine Learning are numerous and diverse, influencing many aspects of daily life. From personalized recommendations on streaming platforms to fraud detection in banking systems, Machine Learning powers many of the intelligent services people rely on today. Its integration into healthcare, transportation, and even creative fields demonstrates its versatility and growing significance as a tool for solving real-world problems.

By learning from data, making predictions, and adapting over time, Machine Learning serves as a cornerstone of modern AI, bridging the gap between raw information and actionable insights in ways that were previously unattainable.

Chapter 4: The Deep Dive Into Deep Learning (DL)

Deep Learning is a specialized branch of Machine Learning that leverages neural networks to simulate the structure and function of the human brain. Neural networks are systems of interconnected nodes, much like neurons in the brain, that work together to process information and make decisions. Each node performs a simple operation on incoming data and passes the result to the next layer, allowing the network to tackle complex tasks by breaking them down into smaller, manageable computations. This architecture enables Deep Learning models to recognize patterns, interpret data, and generate insights with remarkable precision.

The term "deep" in Deep Learning refers to the multiple layers of processing within these neural networks. Unlike traditional Machine Learning models that might operate with a single layer of analysis, Deep Learning models use many layers to extract increasingly abstract features from the data. For instance, in an image recognition system, the first layer might detect simple edges, the next might identify shapes, and subsequent layers might recognize objects like faces or vehicles. By stacking these layers, Deep Learning systems can handle highly complex tasks, making them invaluable for applications like facial recognition, autonomous driving, and speech synthesis.

Deep Learning operates by analyzing data through nodes, connections, and statistical relationships. Each connection between nodes has a weight that determines its influence on the outcome, and these weights are adjusted as the network learns from data. During training, the system evaluates its performance on given tasks and tweaks these weights to improve accuracy. For example, in image recognition, the network might initially misclassify a picture of a cat, but through iterative adjustments, it becomes better at distinguishing cats from other objects. This ability to refine itself through feedback is what makes Deep Learning so powerful.

One of the most impressive aspects of Deep Learning is its ability to tackle complex challenges. In image recognition, it can process millions of pixels to identify intricate patterns and make accurate classifications. Similarly, in speech synthesis, it converts written text into natural-sounding speech by understanding linguistic patterns and context. These capabilities are achieved through vast amounts of training data and the intricate architecture of neural networks, which allow Deep Learning systems to excel in tasks that were once thought to be exclusive to human intelligence.

However, Deep Learning is not without its challenges. One of the most significant issues is the "black box" problem—the lack of transparency in how these systems arrive at their conclusions. While Deep Learning models produce highly accurate results, they often cannot clearly explain the logic behind their decisions. This opacity can make it difficult to trust the outputs of these systems, particularly in critical applications like healthcare or finance, where understanding the rationale is essential.

To address these concerns, researchers are developing methods to measure the reliability and accuracy of Deep Learning systems. By using techniques such as model validation and interpretability tools, they aim to shed light on how these networks function and ensure that their outputs are both dependable and explainable. Despite these efforts, the complexity of Deep Learning models continues to pose challenges in fully understanding and validating their decisions.

Deep Learning stands at the forefront of AI advancements, offering unparalleled capabilities in processing and interpreting complex data. While it opens the door to groundbreaking innovations, its challenges highlight the need for continued research and thoughtful application to harness its potential responsibly.

Chapter 5: The AI Ecosystem

The relationship between Artificial Intelligence, Machine Learning, and Deep Learning can be understood as a layered structure, often represented through a Venn diagram. At the highest level, AI is the superset, encompassing all technologies and systems designed to replicate or enhance human intelligence. Within this broader realm lies Machine Learning, a subset of AI focused specifically on systems that learn and improve through data. Deep Learning, in turn, is a specialized branch of Machine Learning that uses neural networks with multiple layers to process complex patterns and relationships.

This hierarchical relationship is significant because it highlights the interconnectedness of these fields while emphasizing their distinctions.

AI serves as the umbrella term, capturing everything from traditional rule-based systems to the most advanced neural networks. Machine Learning narrows the scope to algorithms that rely on data-driven learning, while Deep Learning delves deeper into leveraging neural networks to handle tasks requiring intricate analysis, such as image recognition or natural language understanding.

Beyond Machine Learning and Deep Learning, AI encompasses other critical fields that expand its capabilities and applications. Natural Language Processing (NLP) is one such area, enabling machines to understand, interpret, and generate human language. NLP powers technologies like chatbots, virtual assistants, and language translation tools, allowing machines to engage with people in meaningful ways. Similarly, computer vision equips systems with the ability to process and interpret visual information, from identifying objects in images to analyzing video feeds for motion detection or facial recognition.

Another essential component of AI is robotics, which integrates intelligent systems with physical motion and interaction. Robotics goes beyond static computation by allowing machines to navigate environments, manipulate objects, and perform tasks that require coordination and precision. From industrial robots assembling products to advanced robots assisting in healthcare or disaster response, this field demonstrates the tangible, real-world applications of AI.

These domains—Machine Learning, Deep Learning, NLP, computer vision, and robotics—are not isolated silos but interconnected disciplines that enhance one another. For instance, a self-driving car relies on computer vision to interpret road conditions, NLP to process voice commands, and Deep Learning to make split-second decisions. The synergy between these fields is what enables AI to achieve its full potential, addressing complex challenges by combining diverse capabilities.

Understanding this interconnected structure underscores the versatility and scope of AI. It is not a singular technology but a multifaceted domain where each subset contributes unique strengths. Together, these fields create a robust framework, pushing the boundaries of what machines can achieve and shaping the future of intelligent systems.

Chapter 6: Real-World Applications of AI

Artificial Intelligence has seamlessly woven itself into our everyday lives, often in ways we take for granted. Voice assistants like Siri, Alexa, and Google Assistant have become household staples, responding to queries, setting reminders, and even controlling smart devices with simple voice commands. Recommendation systems on platforms like Netflix and Amazon use AI to analyze viewing habits or shopping preferences, offering tailored suggestions that enhance user experience. These applications demonstrate how AI, even in its most accessible forms, has become an indispensable tool for convenience and efficiency.

Beyond personal use, AI's impact is profoundly felt across industries. In healthcare, AI-driven diagnostic tools analyze medical images and patient data with remarkable accuracy, aiding doctors in identifying conditions earlier and more effectively. Finance leverages AI to detect fraud, manage risk, and provide personalized investment advice. Manufacturing has seen significant advancements with AI-powered robots streamlining production lines, reducing errors, and increasing efficiency. In entertainment, AI generates realistic visual effects, composes music, and even creates lifelike characters in video games and movies, redefining creativity in the process.

AI's ability to process and analyze vast amounts of data is fundamentally reshaping decision-making processes across fields. It offers businesses actionable insights, helping them optimize operations, anticipate market trends, and improve customer satisfaction. Creativity is also being reimagined, with AI tools enabling designers, writers, and artists to explore new possibilities and push the boundaries of their craft. Productivity gains are equally significant, as automation reduces the time spent on repetitive tasks, allowing professionals to focus on strategic and creative endeavors.

However, the rapid adoption of AI raises important ethical considerations. Privacy remains a pressing issue as AI systems collect and analyze sensitive personal data. Questions about how this data is stored, shared, and used have sparked debates about transparency and user consent. Accountability is another concern, particularly when AI systems make decisions with far-reaching consequences. Determining who is responsible for errors or biases in AI-driven processes is a complex challenge that demands attention. The societal impact of AI, from potential job displacement to the reinforcement of biases in algorithms, further underscores the need for ethical frameworks to guide its development and use.

AI's transformative potential is undeniable, offering unprecedented opportunities for innovation and progress. Yet, as we embrace these advancements, it is crucial to address the ethical implications and ensure that AI is harnessed responsibly. Balancing innovation with accountability will determine the role AI plays in shaping a future that benefits everyone.

Chapter 7: Challenges and Limitations

Despite its remarkable advancements, Artificial Intelligence faces several technical hurdles that limit its potential and raise significant challenges. One of the most prominent issues is the lack of explainability, particularly in deep learning models. These systems often operate as "black boxes," producing accurate outputs without revealing how they arrived at their conclusions. This opacity can be problematic, especially in critical applications like healthcare or criminal justice, where understanding the rationale behind decisions is essential. The inability to explain outcomes not only undermines trust but also makes it difficult to identify errors or biases within the system.

Another major hurdle lies in the reliance on high-quality, diverse datasets. AI systems learn by analyzing data, and their accuracy and fairness depend on the quality of the information they process. Insufficient or biased datasets can lead to flawed models that reinforce existing inequalities or produce unreliable results. For example, an AI model trained on biased data may inadvertently discriminate against certain groups, amplifying systemic issues instead of addressing them. Ensuring that datasets are comprehensive, representative, and free of bias is critical for the development of robust and ethical AI systems.

Human oversight remains a vital component in the management and improvement of AI. While these systems can learn and adapt autonomously, they still require human intervention to guide their training, validate their outputs, and ensure they align with ethical standards. Humans play a crucial role in identifying and mitigating biases that may arise during the development process. Without vigilant oversight, AI algorithms risk perpetuating harmful stereotypes or making decisions that conflict with societal values.

Looking ahead, the future of AI presents both opportunities and challenges. One of the greatest tasks will be balancing the drive for innovation with ethical practices. As AI becomes more powerful, its potential for misuse also grows, necessitating the establishment of clear guidelines and regulatory frameworks. Ensuring that AI technologies are developed responsibly will require collaboration between researchers, policymakers, and industry leaders.

Another challenge lies in preparing for the disruptive impact AI may have on industries and the workforce. While automation and intelligent systems can enhance efficiency and productivity, they may also displace jobs, leading to economic and social upheaval. Addressing these disruptions will require forward-thinking strategies, such as retraining programs and the creation of new roles that leverage the unique capabilities of humans in partnership with AI.

As AI continues to evolve, overcoming these challenges will be essential for realizing its full potential. By addressing technical limitations, fostering ethical practices, and preparing for its societal impact, we can ensure that AI becomes a tool for progress and innovation rather than a source of division or inequality.

Chapter 8: The Future of AI, ML, and DL

Artificial Intelligence is advancing at an unprecedented pace, with innovations in hardware and software pushing its capabilities to new heights. Improvements in AI-specific hardware, such as advanced GPUs and specialized chips like TPUs, have significantly accelerated the processing power needed to train complex models. This hardware evolution is complemented by advancements in software, with more efficient algorithms enabling faster learning, greater accuracy, and the ability to handle increasingly large datasets. Together, these developments are making AI systems more accessible, scalable, and versatile than ever before.

The integration of AI with emerging technologies like quantum computing holds the promise of transformative breakthroughs. Quantum computing, with its ability to perform calculations at speeds far beyond traditional computers, could revolutionize AI by solving problems that are currently infeasible due to computational constraints. From optimizing supply chains to advancing drug discovery, the synergy between AI and quantum computing has the potential to tackle challenges on a scale previously unimaginable.

Looking ahead, the next decade will see AI continuing to reshape both business and everyday life. In the corporate world, AI is expected to enhance decision-making, automate complex processes, and unlock new business models. Personalized marketing, predictive analytics, and intelligent customer support will become even more refined, driving efficiency and customer satisfaction. On a personal level, AI will integrate further into daily routines, from smart home systems that anticipate our needs to wearable devices that monitor health in real time.

However, the implications of AI extend beyond convenience and efficiency; it could fundamentally redefine the workforce and society. As automation takes over repetitive and mundane tasks, humans will have the opportunity to focus on creativity, strategy, and innovation. Yet this shift will also require significant adaptation. Many traditional jobs may disappear, creating a pressing need for education and retraining programs to prepare the workforce for AI-driven industries. Addressing this transition will be critical to ensuring that the benefits of AI are shared broadly and equitably.

The opportunities AI presents are immense, offering the potential to solve some of the world's most pressing challenges. From combating climate change with predictive analytics to improving global healthcare systems through early diagnosis and personalized treatment, AI-driven solutions could bring about significant positive change. Yet, these opportunities come with risks that cannot be overlooked. Concerns about control and over-reliance on automation highlight the importance of maintaining human oversight and ensuring that AI systems are aligned with ethical standards. Striking the right balance between harnessing AI's power and safeguarding against its unintended consequences will be one of the defining challenges of this era.

AI's future is full of promise, but it also demands responsibility and foresight. By advancing the technology thoughtfully and addressing its societal impacts proactively, we can unlock its potential to create a smarter, more equitable world while mitigating the risks it brings.

Conclusion

Artificial Intelligence, Machine Learning, and Deep Learning represent a continuum of innovation, each contributing uniquely to the evolution of intelligent systems. AI serves as the overarching domain, encompassing a wide range of capabilities that aim to replicate or surpass human intelligence. Machine Learning, a subset of AI, focuses on enabling systems to learn from data, while Deep Learning, as a specialized subset of Machine Learning, leverages neural networks to tackle some of the most complex tasks. Understanding these distinctions and their interconnectedness is crucial for appreciating how these technologies work together to drive advancements in various fields.

The growing presence of AI in our lives underscores the importance of deepening our understanding of these technologies. They are not just tools for experts; they are transformative forces shaping industries, redefining workflows, and influencing decisions that impact us all. From personalized recommendations to life-saving applications in healthcare, AI, ML, and DL are reshaping the way we live, work, and solve problems. Familiarizing ourselves with these technologies empowers us to engage with them meaningfully, whether as professionals, consumers, or informed citizens.

As AI continues to evolve, its impact will only grow, bringing both opportunities and challenges. The key to navigating this future lies in embracing a mindset of lifelong learning. Staying informed about the latest developments in AI ensures that we remain prepared for its implications, whether it's adapting to changes in the workplace or leveraging AI tools to solve complex problems. By understanding AI's capabilities and limitations, we can approach its applications with confidence and critical thinking.

Embracing knowledge about AI is not just an academic exercise; it is a practical necessity in a world where intelligent systems are increasingly integral to progress. The future will belong to those who can harness the potential of AI responsibly, balancing its transformative power with ethical considerations. By fostering awareness and curiosity, we can position ourselves to thrive in an AI-driven era and contribute to shaping a future where technology serves humanity's best interests.

www.ingramcontent.com/pod-product-compliance
Lightning Source LLC
LaVergne TN
LVHW051625050326
832903LV00033B/4672